GARFIELD

Classics

Volume Seventeen

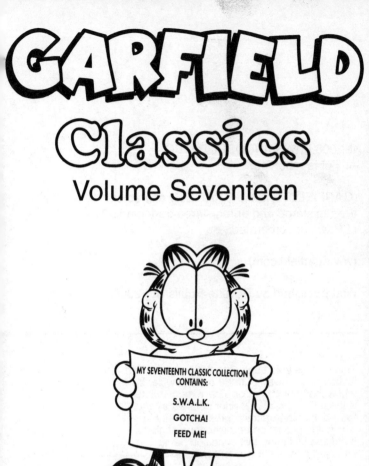

MY SEVENTEENTH CLASSIC COLLECTION
CONTAINS:

S.W.A.L.K.

GOTCHA!

FEED ME!

JiM DAViS

First published by Ravette Publishing 2006.

Printed and bound in Great Britain
for Ravette Publishing Limited,
Unit 3, Tristar Centre,
Star Road, Partridge Green,
West Sussex RH13 8RA

ISBN 10: 1-84161-250-2
ISBN 13: 978-1-84161-250-8

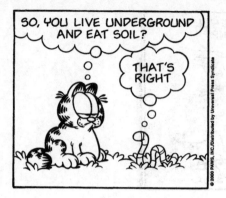

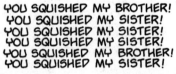

JIM DAVIS 12-20

www.garfield.com

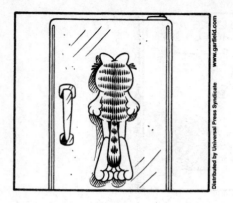

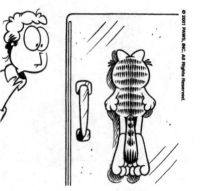

IS IT POSSIBLE THAT I'VE LOST THE ELEMENT OF SURPRISE?

JIM DAVIS 2-7

TOMORROW I'M GOING BACK TO GETTING DRESSED AFTER I TAKE MY SHOWER!

WELL, AT LEAST YOU TRIED SOMETHING

Feed Me!

JiM DAVIS

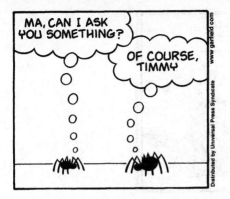

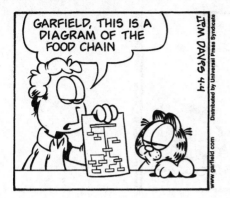

JIM DAVIS 4-5

THE SECRET TO LOOKING
GOOD IS TO ACCESSORIZE

IT'S NICE WHEN GARFIELD'S ASLEEP. HE CAN'T ANNOY ME

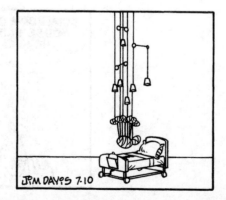

7-12

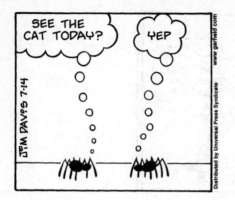

OTHER GARFIELD BOOKS AVAILABLE

Pocket Books		Price	ISBN
Below Par		£3.50	1 84161 152 2
Compute This!		£3.50	1 84161 194 8
Don't Ask!	(new)	£3.99	1 84161 247 2
Double Trouble		£3.50	1 84161 008 9
Feed Me!		£3.99	1 84161 242 1
Gotcha!		£3.50	1 84161 226 X
I Am What I Am!		£3.99	1 84161 243 X
I Don't Do Perky		£3.50	1 84161 195 6
Kowabunga!	(new)	£3.99	1 84161 246 4
Light Of My Life		£3.50	1 85304 353 2
Pop Star		£3.50	1 84161 151 4
S.W.A.L.K.		£3.50	1 84161 225 1

new titles available Feb 07

No.55 - Wan2tlk?		£3.99	1 84161 264 2
No.56 - Get Serious		£3.99	1 84161 265 0

Theme Books	Price	ISBN
Behaving Badly	£4.50	1 85304 892 5
Cat Napping	£4.50	1 84161 087 9
Coffee Mornings	£4.50	1 84161 086 0
Creatures Great & Small	£3.99	1 85304 998 0
Entertains You	£4.50	1 84161 221 9
Healthy Living	£3.99	1 85304 972 7
Pigging Out	£4.50	1 85304 893 3
Slam Dunk!	£4.50	1 84161 222 7
Successful Living	£3.99	1 85304 973 5
The Seasons	£3.99	1 85304 999 9

2-in-1 Theme Books	Price	ISBN
All In Good Taste	£6.99	1 84161 209 X
Easy Does It	£6.99	1 84161 191 3
Lazy Daze	£6.99	1 84161 208 1
Licensed to Thrill	£6.99	1 84161 192 1
Out For The Couch	£6.99	1 84161 144 1
The Gruesome Twosome	£6.99	1 84161 143 3

Classics	Price	ISBN
Volume One	£6.99	1 85304 970 0
Volume Two	£5.99	1 85304 971 9
Volume Three	£5.99	1 85304 996 4
Volume Four	£6.99	1 85304 997 2
Volume Five	£6.99	1 84161 022 4
Volume Six	£6.99	1 84161 023 2
Volume Seven	£5.99	1 84161 088 7
Volume Eight	£5.99	1 84161 089 5

Classics (cont'd ...)		Price	ISBN
Volume Nine		£6.99	1 84161 149 2
Volume Ten		£6.99	1 84161 150 6
Volume Eleven		£6.99	1 84161 175 1
Volume Twelve		£6.99	1 84161 176 X
Volume Thirteen		£5.99	1 84161 206 5
Volume Fourteen		£6.99	1 84161 207 3
Volume Fifteen		£5.99	1 84161 232 4
Volume Sixteen		£5.99	1 84161 233 2
Volume Eighteen	(new)	£6.99	1 84161 251 0
Little Books			
C-c-c-caffeine		£2.50	1 84161 183 2
Food 'n' Fitness		£2.50	1 84161 145 X
Laughs		£2.50	1 84161 146 8
Love 'n' Stuff		£2.50	1 84161 147 6
Surf 'n' Sun		£2.50	1 84161 186 7
The Office		£2.50	1 84161 184 0
Zzzzzz		£2.50	1 84161 185 9
Miscellaneous			
Garfield 25 years of me!		£7.99	1 84161 173 5
Treasury 7	(new)	£10.99	1 84161 248 0
Treasury 6		£10.99	1 84161 229 4
Treasury 5		£10.99	1 84161 198 0
Treasury 4		£10.99	1 84161 180 8
Treasury 3		£9.99	1 84161 142 5

All Garfield books are available at your local bookshop or from the publisher at the address below. Just tick the titles required and send the form with your payment to:-

RAVETTE PUBLISHING
Unit 3, Tristar Centre, Star Road, Partridge Green, West Sussex RH13 8RA

Prices and availability are subject to change without notice.

Please enclose a cheque or postal order made payable to **Ravette Publishing** to the value of the cover price of the book/s and allow the following for UK postage and packing:-

70p for the first book + 40p for each additional book
except Garfield Treasuries ... when please add £3.00 per copy for p&p.

Name ....

Address ....

....

....